SPURGEON'S
Catechism

By Charles Spurgeon

Revised and Updated by Roger McReynolds

Also Updated Into Modern English
(using the English Standard Version unless otherwise indicated)

Charles Haddon Spurgeon
General Works

According to Promise: The Lord's Method of Dealing with His Chosen People

All of Grace (in 12-point and Large Print 16-point font paperback editions)

All of Grace (using the Christian Standard Bible—CSB)

Peace and Purpose in Trial and Suffering

The Clue of the Maze: 70 Daily Readings for Conquering Doubt + 3 Sermons on Doubting

Devotionals

The New Spurgeon's Devotional Bible: A 600,000 Word Two Year Devotional

Evening by Evening (using the Christian Standard Bible—CSB)

Morning by Morning (using the Christian Standard Bible—CSB)

Most Things Spurgeon: A One Year Daily Devotional

John Ploughman

John Ploughman's Everyday Advice

John Ploughman's Talk

Commentaries

Matthew The Gospel of the Kingdom Expanded

Spurgeon's Commentary on Psalms Volume 1 | Psalm 1-57

Spurgeon's Commentary on Psalms Volume 2 | Psalm 58-110 (2022)

Spurgeon's Commentary on Psalms Volume 3 | Psalm 111-150 (2023)

The Imprecatory Psalms from The Treasury of David (including Explanatory Notes)

The Penitential Psalms from The Treasury of David (including Explanatory Notes)

Ministry

Come, O Children

Lectures to My Students Volume One

Lectures to My Students Volume Two (2022)

Lectures to My Students Volumes Three & Four (Combined • 2024)

Spurgeon's Catechism: Updated for Today's Readers with Proof Texts in the ESV

The Soul Winner

Spurgeon's Sermons Series

3:16: Thirteen Selected Sermons

A Defense of Calvinism: Including 7 Sermons on the Doctrines of Grace

A Sower Went Out to Sow: Nine Sermons on The Parable of the Sower

Lessons From Jonah

Lost and Found: 10 Evangelistic Sermons

The Prodigal Son and Other Parables of Jesus

Other Works

Sermons of D. L. Moody: 21 Sermons

The Fear of God, by John Bunyan

The Reformed Pastor, by Richard Baxter

View descriptions for all eBooks, Print Books, and Audio Books, and download Free chapters, at **RogerMcR.com**

Contact Information

MostThingsSpurgeon@gmail.com

Foreword and Acknowledgments

The catechisms Mr. Spurgeon was referring to (see Introduction) are the Westminster Shorter Catechism (1647) and a Baptist catechism based on the London Baptist Confession (1689). He did this in 1855, the year he turned twenty-one.

Once more, my sincere thanks to our faithful team. My wife, Patti, works through my first draft, making suggestions to make sure it truly is "Updated for Today's Reader." Next, my sister, Laura, puts her three degrees to work, proofreading to improve my grammar and vocabulary. Our daughter, Amber Smart, designs the covers and formats the interiors of all our books.

And a special Thank You to my young friend David Rodriguez, who very willingly worked through this catechism with me week by week, and pointed out some ways to improve it. I was always so pleased that you still had the answers from the week before memorized.

.

INTRODUCTION

I am convinced that the use of a good catechism in all our families will be a great defense against the increasing errors of the times. Therefore, I have put together this little manual from the Westminster Assembly's and Baptist Catechisms, for the use of my own church and congregation. Those who use it in their families or classes must work hard to explain the meaning to the little ones; but the words should be carefully learned by heart; they will be understood better as the child grows older.

May the Lord bless my dear friends and their families always, is the prayer of their loving Pastor.

—C. H. Spurgeon

QUESTIONS

1.   What is the main reason a person exists?

2.   What rule has God given to show us how we may glorify and enjoy him?

3.   What do the Scriptures teach above all else?

4.   What is God?

5.   Is there more than one God?

6.   How many persons are there in the Godhead?

7.   What are the decrees of God?

8.   How does God carry out his decrees?

9.   What is the work of creation?

10.   How did God create man?

11.   What are God's works of providence?

12.   What special command did God give man when he created him and put him in the garden of Eden?

13.   Did our first parents continue to live in the condition in which they were created?

14.   What is sin?

15.   Did all humanity fall in Adam's first sin?

16.   Into what condition did the fall bring humanity?

17.   What is included in the sinful life into which humanity has fallen?

18.   What unhappiness resulted from humanity's fall?

19.   Did God leave all humanity to suffer death in their state of sin and hopelessness?

20.   Did God leave all humanity to suffer death in their state of sin and hopelessness?

21.   How did Christ, being the Son of God, become man?

44. Which is the second commandment?

45. What is required in the second commandment?

46. What is forbidden in the second commandment?

47. Which is the third commandment?

48. What is required in the third commandment?

49. Which is the fourth commandment?

50. What is required in the fourth commandment?

51. How is the Sabbath to be kept separate?

52. Which is the fifth commandment?

53. What is required in the fifth commandment?

54. What reason are we given for obeying the fifth commandment?

55. Which is the sixth commandment?

56. What is forbidden in the sixth commandment?

57. Which is the seventh commandment?

58. What is forbidden in the seventh commandment?

59. Which is the eighth commandment?

60. What is forbidden in the eighth commandment?

61. Which is the ninth commandment?

62. What is required in the ninth commandment?

63. Which is the tenth commandment?

64. What is forbidden in the tenth commandment?

65. Is any person able to keep the commandments of God perfectly?

66. Is all breaking of the law equally wicked?

67. What does every sin deserve?

68. How may we escape the anger and curse of God that we deserve due to our sin?

69. What is faith in Jesus Christ?

70. What is repentance that leads to life?

71. What are the external and normal ways the Holy Spirit uses to give us the benefits of Christ's redemption?

72. How is the Word of God used to achieve salvation?

73. How is the Word of God to be read and heard to achieve salvation?

74. How do baptism and the Lord's Supper become effective instruments of grace?

75. What is baptism?

76. Who may be baptized?

77. Are the infants of parents who claim to be Christians to be baptized?

78. How is baptism correctly performed?

79. What is the responsibility of those who are baptized according to the will of God?

80. What is the Lord's Supper?

81. What is required to participate in the Lord's Supper?

82. What is meant by the words, "until he comes," that are used by the apostle Paul regarding the Lord's Supper?

QUESTION #1

What is the main reason a person exists?

The main reason a person exists is to glorify* God,[1] and to enjoy him forever.[2]

[1] So, whether you eat or drink, or whatever you do, do all to the glory of God.

—1 Corinthians 10:31

[2] Whom have I in heaven but you? And there is nothing on earth that I desire besides you. My flesh and my heart may fail, but God is the strength of my heart and my portion forever.

—Psalm 73:25-26

* *glorify* — to praise, honor in worship, honor in thoughts or words, adore, give thanks to.

QUESTION #2

What rule has God given to teach us how we may glorify and enjoy him?

The Word of God that is contained in the Scriptures of the Old and New Testaments[1] is the only rule to teach us how we may glorify God and enjoy him.[2]

[1] [You are] built on the foundation of the apostles and prophets, Christ Jesus himself being the cornerstone.

—Ephesians 2:20

All Scripture is breathed out by God and profitable for teaching, for reproof, for correction, and for training in righteousness.

—2 Timothy 3:16

[2] That which we have seen and heard we proclaim also to you, so that you too may have fellowship with us; and indeed our fellowship is with the Father and with his Son Jesus Christ.

—1 John 1:3

QUESTION #3

What do the Scriptures teach people above all else?

Above all else the Scriptures teach people what to believe about God, and what commitment God requires of them.[1]

[1] Follow the pattern of the sound words that you have heard from me, in the faith and love that are in Christ Jesus.
—2 Timothy 1:13

The end of the matter; all has been heard. Fear God and keep his commandments, for this is the whole duty of man.
—Ecclesiastes 12:13

QUESTION #4

What is God?

God is a Spirit.[1] He is infinite,[2] eternal,[3] and unchangeable[4] in his being,[5] wisdom, power,[6] holiness,[7] justice, goodness, and truth.[8]

[1] God is spirit.　　　　　　　　　　　　　　　—John 4:24

[2] Can you find out the deep things of God? Can you find out the limit of the Almighty?

　　　　　　　　　　　　　　　—Job 11:7

[3] From everlasting to everlasting you are God.

　　　　　　　　　　　　　　　—Psalm 90:2

To the King of the ages, immortal, invisible, the only God, be honor and glory forever and ever. Amen.

　　　　　　　　　　　　　　　—1 Timothy 1:17

[4] The Father of lights, with whom there is no variation or shadow due to change.

　　　　　　　　　　　　　　　—James 1:17

[5] God said to Moses, "I AM WHO I AM." And he said, "Say this to the people of Israel: 'I AM has sent me to you.'"

　　　　　　　　　　　　　　　—Exodus 3:14

[6] Great is our Lord, and abundant in power; his understanding is beyond measure.

　　　　　　　　　　　　　　　—Psalm 147:5

[7] Holy, holy, holy, is the Lord God Almighty, who was and is and is to come!

　　　　　　　　　　　　　　　—Revelation 4:8

[8] The Lord, the Lord, a God merciful and gracious, slow to anger, and abounding in steadfast love and faithfulness, keeping steadfast love for thousands, forgiving iniquity and transgression and sin, but who will by no means clear the guilty.

　　　　　　　　　　　　　　　—Exodus 34:6-7

QUESTION #5

Is there more than one God?

There is only one God,[1] the living and true God.[2]

[1] Hear, O Israel: The LORD our God, the LORD is one.

—Deuteronomy 6:4

[2] The LORD is the true God; he is the living God.

—Jeremiah 10:10

How many persons are there in the Godhead?

There are three persons in the Godhead, the Father, the Son, and the Holy Spirit, and these three are one God, the same in essence, equal in power and glory.[1]

> [1] Go therefore and make disciples of all nations, baptizing them in the name of the Father and of the Son and of the Holy Spirit.
>
> —Matthew 28:19

> The grace of the Lord Jesus Christ and the love of God and the fellowship of the Holy Spirit be with you all.
>
> —2 Corinthians 13:14

What are the decrees* of God?

The decrees* of God are his eternal purpose, according to the counsel of his own will, where for his own glory he has foreordained** whatever happens.[1]

> [1]In him we have obtained an inheritance, having been predestined according to the purpose of him who works all things according to the counsel of his will, so that we who were the first to hope in Christ might be to the praise of his glory.
>
> —Ephesians 1:11-12

* *decree* — an official order issued by a legal authority, the legal ruling of a judge. "In those days a *decree* went out from Caesar Augustus that all the world should be registered" (Luke 2:1). God has predetermined, for his own glory, everything that will happen.

** *foreordain* — to ordain, appoint, or decree beforehand; to predestinate; to predetermine.

How does God carry out his decrees?

God carries out his decrees through the works of creation[1] and providence.[2]*

[1] You created all things and by your will they existed and were created.

—Revelation 4:11

[2] He does according to his will among the host of heaven and among the inhabitants of the earth.

—Daniel 4:35

* *providence* — refers to God's will, his divine intervention, and his predetermination (predestination).

What is the work of creation?

The work of creation is God's making all things[1] from nothing, by the word of his power,[2] in six days, and seeing that it was good. [3]

[1]In the beginning, God created the heavens and the earth.

—Genesis 1:1

[2]By faith we understand that the universe was created by the word of God, so that what is seen was not made out of things that are visible.

—Hebrews 11:3

[3] For in six days the LORD made heaven and earth, the sea, and all that is in them.

—Exodus 20:11

How did God create man?

God created man male and female, after his own image,[1] in knowledge, righteousness and holiness,[2] with supreme authority over his creation.[3]

[1] So God created man in his own image, in the image of God he created him; male and female he created them.

—Genesis 1:27

[2] And have put on the new self, which is being renewed in knowledge after the image of its creator.

—Colossians 3:10

And to put on the new self, created after the likeness of God in true righteousness and holiness.

—Ephesians 4:24

[3] And God blessed them. And God said to them, "Be fruitful and multiply and fill the earth and subdue it, and have dominion over the fish of the sea and over the birds of the heavens and over every living thing that moves on the earth."

—Genesis 1:28

QUESTION #11

What are God's works of providence?

God's works of providence are his most holy,[1] wise,[2] and powerful upholding[3] and ruling over all his creatures, and all of their actions.[4]

[1] The LORD our God is holy!

—Psalm 99:9

The LORD is righteous in all his ways and kind in all his works.

—Psalm 145:17

[2] This also comes from the LORD of hosts; he is wonderful in counsel and excellent in wisdom.

—Isaiah 28:29

[3] He upholds the universe by the word of his power.

—Hebrews 1:3

You preserve [sustain, maintain] all of them.

—Nehemiah 9:6

[4] His kingdom rules over all.

—Psalm 103:19

Are not two sparrows sold for a penny? And not one of them will fall to the ground apart from your Father.
—Matthew 10:29

QUESTION #12

What special command did God give man when he created him and put him in the garden of Eden?

When God created man, he entered into a covenant* of life with him, on the condition that he would obey perfectly;[1] he banned him from eating of the tree of the knowledge of good and evil, on pain of death.[2]

[1]But the law is not of faith, rather "The one who does them shall live by them."

—Galatians 3:12

[2] But of the tree of the knowledge of good and evil you shall not eat, for in the day that you eat of it you shall surely die."

—Genesis 2:17

* *covenant* — a formal agreement between two or more parties, a contract, a promise.

Did our first parents continue to live in the condition in which they were created?

Our first parents were left to the freedom of their own will, but fell from their position by sinning against God,[1] by eating the forbidden fruit.[2]

[1] God made man upright, but they have sought out many schemes.
—Ecclesiastes 7:29

[2] When the woman saw that the tree was good for food, and that it was a delight to the eyes, and that the tree was to be desired to make one wise, she took of its fruit and ate, and she also gave some to her husband who was with her, and he ate. Then the eyes of both were opened, and they knew that they were naked…. And they heard the sound of the LORD God walking in the garden in the cool of the day, and the man and his wife hid themselves from the presence of the LORD God among the trees of the garden.
—Genesis 3:6-8

What is sin?

Sin is any lack of conforming to, or breaking of, the law of God.[1]

[1] Everyone who makes a practice of sinning also practices lawlessness; sin is lawlessness.
                              —1 John 3:4

Did all humanity fall in Adam's first sin?

The covenant made with Adam included not only himself but all his descendants. All of Adam's offspring sinned in him and fell with him in his first sin.[1]

[1] For as in Adam all die, so also in Christ shall all be made alive.
—1 Corinthians 15:22

Therefore, just as sin came into the world through one man, and death through sin, and so death spread to all men because all sinned.
—Romans 5:12

Into what condition did the fall bring humanity?

The fall brought humanity into a state of sin and misery.[1]

[1] One trespass led to condemnation for all men.
—Romans 5:18

QUESTION #17

What is included in the sinful life into which humanity has fallen?

The sinful life into which humanity has fallen, consists of the guilt of Adam's first sin,[1] the lack of original righteousness,[2] and the corruption of their whole nature, which is generally called original sin,[3] together with all actual sins that proceed from it. [4]

[1] For as by the one man's disobedience the many were made sinners.

—Romans 5:19

[2] None is righteous, no, not one.

—Romans 3:10

[3] And you were dead in the trespasses and sins.

—Ephesians 2:1

Behold, I was brought forth in iniquity, and in sin did my mother conceive me.

—Psalm 51:5

[4] For out of the heart come evil thoughts, murder, adultery, sexual immorality, theft, false witness, slander.

—Matthew 15:19

QUESTION #18

What unhappiness resulted from humanity's fall?

By their fall, all humanity lost fellowship with God,[1] are under his wrath and curse,[2] are responsible for all their unhappiness in this life, for death itself, and for all the pains of hell forever.[3]

[1] [Adam] and his wife hid themselves from the presence of the LORD God among the trees of the garden...[so] he drove out the man.

—Genesis 3:8, 24

[2] We...were by nature children of wrath.

—Ephesians 2:3

For it is written, "Cursed be everyone who does not abide by all things written in the Book of the Law, and do them."

—Galatians 3:10

[3] The wages of sin is death.

—Romans 6:23

Then he will say to those on his left, "Depart from me, you cursed, into the eternal fire prepared for the devil and his angels."

—Matthew 25:41

QUESTION #19

Did God leave all humanity to suffer death in their state of sin and hopelessness?

God, having only from his good pleasure from eternity past, elected some to eternal life,[1] entered into a covenant of grace to deliver them from their state of sin and hopelessness and bring them into a state of salvation by a Redeemer.[2]

[1] God chose you from the beginning to be saved, through sanctification by the Spirit and belief in the truth.

—2 Thessalonians 2:13 (alternate reading)

[2] So that, as sin reigned in death, grace also might reign through righteousness leading to eternal life through Jesus Christ our Lord.

—Romans 5:21

QUESTION #20

Who is the Redeemer of God's elect?

The only Redeemer of God's elect is the Lord Jesus Christ,[1] who being the eternal Son of God, became man,[2] and was and continues to be God and man, in two distinct natures, and one person forever.[3]

[1] For there is one God, and there is one mediator between God and men, the man Christ Jesus.

—2 Timothy 2:5

[2] The Word became flesh and dwelt among us.

—John 1:14

[3] [God] was manifested in the flesh, vindicated by the Spirit, seen by angels, proclaimed among the nations, believed on in the world, taken up in glory.

—1 Timothy 3:16

For in him the whole fullness of deity dwells bodily.
—Colossians 2:9

Question #21

How did Christ, being the Son of God, become man?

Christ, the Son of God, became man by accepting a true body,[1] and a neutral soul,[2*] being conceived by the power of the Holy Spirit in the womb of the Virgin Mary, and given birth by her,[3] yet without sin.[4]

[1] Since therefore the children share in flesh and blood, he himself likewise partook of the same things.

—Hebrews 2:14

[2] Then he said to them, "My soul is very sorrowful, even to death."

—Matthew 26:38

For we do not have a high priest who is unable to sympathize with our weaknesses, but one who in every respect has been tempted as we are, yet without sin.

—Hebrews 4:15

[3] Behold, you will conceive in your womb and bear a son, and you shall call his name Jesus.... The Holy Spirit will come upon you, and the power of the Most High will overshadow you.

—Luke 1:31, 35

[4] For it was indeed fitting that we should have such a high priest, holy, innocent, unstained, separated from sinners.

—Hebrews 7:26

* *neutral soul* — a soul like Adam's before the fall.

What duties does Christ fulfill as our Redeemer?

Christ, as our Redeemer, fulfills the duties of a prophet,[1] of a priest,[2] and of a king,[3] in both his state of humiliation and exaltation.

[1] Moses said, "The Lord God will raise up for you a prophet like me from your brothers. You shall listen to him in whatever he tells you."

—Acts 3:22

[2] You are a priest forever, after the order of Melchizedek.

—Hebrews 5:6

[3] As for me, I have set my King on Zion, my holy hill.

—Psalm 2:6

How does Christ fulfill the office of a prophet?

Christ fulfills the office of a prophet by showing us,[1] through the Bible [2] and the Holy Spirit,[3] God's will for our salvation.

[1] No one has ever seen God; the only God, who is at the Father's side, he has made him known.

—John 1:18

[2] These are written so that you may believe that Jesus is the Christ, the Son of God, and that by believing you may have life in his name.

—John 20:31

[3] The Helper, the Holy Spirit, whom the Father will send in my name, he will teach you all things.

—John 14:26

How does Christ fulfill the office of a priest?

Christ fulfills the office of a priest by offering himself only one time as a sacrifice to satisfy God's justice,[1] restoring us to God,[2] and by continually praying for us.[3]

[1] Christ, having been offered once to bear the sins of many…

—Hebrews 9:28

[2] Therefore he had to be made like his brothers in every respect, so that he might become a merciful and faithful high priest in the service of God, to make propitiation* for the sins of the people.

—Hebrews 2:17

[3] He is able to save to the uttermost those who draw near to God through him, since he always lives to make intercession** for them.

—Hebrews 7:25

* *propitiation* — The act of satisfying someone's demands and changing that someone from an enemy into a friend. When Jesus Christ died on the cross he satisfied the demand of God the Father that a sacrifice for sin must be made to him. The wrath or anger of God was used up on Christ so that God's justice was satisfied and we who were once the enemies of God became his friends.

** *intercession* — prayer to God for, or on behalf of, someone else.

QUESTION #25

How does Christ fulfill the office of a king?

Christ fulfills the office of a king by changing our wills to serve him,[1] by ruling and defending us,[2] and in suppressing and conquering all his and our enemies.

[1] Your people will offer themselves freely, on the day of your power.

—Psalm 110:3

[2] From you shall come forth for me one who is to be ruler in Israel.

—Micah 5:2

For he must reign until he has put all his enemies under his feet.
—1 Corinthians 15:25

What does Christ's humiliation include?

Christ's humiliation includes his being born, being born in poor conditions,[1] being made under the law,[2] experiencing the miseries of this life,[3] coming under the wrath of God[4] and the curse of death on the cross,[5] and being buried and continuing under the power of death for a time.[6]

[1] And she gave birth to her firstborn son and wrapped him in swaddling cloths and laid him in a manger.

—Luke 2:7

[2] God sent forth his Son, born of woman, born under the law.

—Galatians 4:4

[3] He was despised and rejected by men, a man of sorrows and acquainted with grief.

—Isaiah 53:3

[4] And about the ninth hour Jesus cried out with a loud voice, saying…, "My God, my God, why have you forsaken me?"

—Matthew 27:46

[5] He humbled himself by becoming obedient to the point of death, even death on a cross.

—Philippians 2:8

[6] For just as Jonah was three days and three nights in the belly of the great fish, so will the Son of Man be three days and three nights in the heart of the earth.

—Matthew 12:40

QUESTION #27

What does Christ's exaltation include?

Christ's exaltation includes his rising from the dead on the third day,[1] his ascending up into heaven, his sitting at the right hand of God the Father,[2] and in his coming to judge the world at the last day.[3]

[1] That he was buried, that he was raised on the third day in accordance with the Scriptures.

—1 Corinthians 15:4

[2] So then the Lord Jesus, after he had spoken to them, was taken up into heaven and sat down at the right hand of God.

—Mark 16.19

[3] He has fixed a day on which he will judge the world in righteousness by a man whom he has appointed; and of this he has given assurance to all by raising him from the dead.

—Acts 17:31

How do we have a part in the redemption purchased by Christ?

We have a part in the redemption purchased by Christ, by the effective work of his Holy Spirit[1] in us.[2]

[1] He saved us, not because of works done by us in righteousness, but according to his own mercy, by the washing of regeneration and renewal of the Holy Spirit, whom he poured out on us richly through Jesus Christ our Savior.

—Titus 3:5-6

[2] To all who did receive him, who believed in his name, he gave the right to become children of God.

—John 1:12

QUESTION #29

How does the Holy Spirit make the redemption purchased by
Christ apply to us?

The Holy Spirit makes the redemption purchased by Christ apply
to us, by creating faith in us,[1] resulting in uniting us to Christ
through our effective calling.[2]

[1] For by grace you have been saved through faith. And this is not
your own doing; it is the gift of God.

—Ephesians 2:8

[2] That Christ may dwell in your hearts through faith.

—Ephesians 3:17

QUESTION #30

What is effective calling?

Effective calling is the work of God's Spirit,[1] by which he persuades and enables us to accept Jesus Christ as freely offered to us in the gospel.[2] The Holy Spirit does this by convincing us of our sin and unhappiness,[3] making the knowledge of Christ clear,[4] and changing our wills.[5]

[1] Who saved us and called us with a holy calling.

—2 Timothy 1:9 (alternate reading)

[2] No one can come to me unless the Father who sent me draws him.... Everyone who has heard and learned from the Father comes to me.

—John 6:44-45

[3] Now when they heard this they were cut to the heart, and said to Peter and the rest of the apostles, "Brothers, what shall we do?"

—Acts 2:37

[4] To open their eyes, so that they may turn from darkness to light and from the power of Satan to God.

—Acts 26:18

[5] I will remove the heart of stone from your flesh and give you a heart of flesh.

—Ezekiel 36:26

QUESTION #31

What benefits do those who are effectively called receive in this life?

Those who are effectively called receive in this life justification,[1] adoption,[2] sanctification, and the distinct benefits that either accompany them or flow from them.[3]

> [1] Those whom he predestined he also called, and those whom he called he also justified, and those whom he justified he also glorified.
>
> —Romans 8:30

> [2] He predestined us for adoption to himself as sons through Jesus Christ.
>
> —Ephesians 1:5

> [3] And because of him you are in Christ Jesus, who became to us wisdom from God, righteousness and sanctification and redemption.
>
> —1 Corinthians 1:30

QUESTION #32

What is justification?

Justification is an act of God's free grace, where he pardons all our sins[1] and accepts us as righteous in his sight,[2] only because of the righteousness Christ credits to us,[3] which is received by faith alone.[4]

[1] For all who believe…are justified by his grace as a gift, through the redemption that is in Christ Jesus.

—Romans 3:24

In him we have redemption through his blood, the forgiveness of our trespasses, according to the riches of his grace.

—Ephesians 1:7

[2] For our sake he made him to be sin who knew no sin, so that in him we might become the righteousness of God.

—2 Corinthians 5:21

[3] For as by the one man's disobedience the many were made sinners, so by the one man's obedience the many will be made righteous.

—Romans 5:19

[4] We know that a person is not justified by works of the law but through faith in Jesus Christ, so we also have believed in Christ Jesus, in order to be justified by faith in Christ.

—Galatians 2:16

And be found in him, not having a righteousness of my own that comes from the law, but that which comes through faith in Christ, the righteousness from God that depends on faith.

—Philippians 3:9

QUESTION #33

What is adoption?

Adoption is an act of God's free grace,[1] where we are received into the family of God, and, as his children, have a right to all the privileges of family members.[2]

[1] See what kind of love the Father has given to us, that we should be called children of God.

—1 John 3:1

[2] But to all who did receive him, who believed in his name, he gave the right to become children of God.

—John 1:12

If children, then heirs—heirs of God and fellow heirs with Christ.

—Romans 8:17

What is sanctification?

Sanctification is the work of God's Spirit,[1] where we are made new again in the image of God,[2] made able to increasingly die to sin, and live a holier life.[3]

[1] God chose you as the firstfruits to be saved, through sanctification by the Spirit.

—2 Thessalonians 2:13

[2] And to put on the new self, created after the likeness of God in true righteousness and holiness.

—Ephesians 4:24

[3] For the death he died he died to sin, once for all, but the life he lives he lives to God. So you also must consider yourselves dead to sin and alive to God in Christ Jesus.

—Romans 6:10-11

What are the benefits in this life that flow or result from justification, adoption, and sanctification?

The benefits in this life that flow or result from justification,[1] adoption and sanctification, are assurance of God's love, peace of conscience, joy in the Holy Spirit,[2] and increase in grace; all of which continue to the end.[3]

[1] Therefore, since we have been justified by faith, we have peace with God through our Lord Jesus Christ. Through him we have also obtained access by faith into this grace in which we stand, and we rejoice in hope of the glory of God.... Hope does not put us to shame, because God's love has been poured into our hearts through the Holy Spirit who has been given to us.

—Romans 5:1-2, 5

[2] For the kingdom of God is not a matter of eating and drinking but of righteousness and peace and joy in the Holy Spirit.

—Romans 14:17

[3] The path of the righteous is like the light of dawn, which shines brighter and brighter until full day.

—Proverbs 4:18

I write these things to you who believe in the name of the Son of God, that you may know that you have eternal life.

—1 John 5:13

Who by God's power are being guarded through faith for a salvation ready to be revealed in the last time.

—1 Peter 1:5

QUESTION #36

What benefits do believers receive from Christ when they die?

The souls of believers are made perfect[1] when they die and are immediately in heaven with the Lord,[2] and their bodies, being still one with Christ,[3] rest in their graves[4] until the resurrection.[5]

[1] To the spirits of the righteous made perfect.

—Hebrews 12:23

[2] My desire is to depart and be with Christ.

—Philippians 1:23

Yes, we are of good courage, and we would rather be away from the body and at home with the Lord.

—2 Corinthians 5:8

Today you will be with me in paradise.

—Luke 23:43

[3] God will bring with him those who have fallen asleep.

—1 Thessalonians 4:14

[4] He enters into peace; they rest in their beds who walk in their uprightness.

—Isaiah 57:2

[5] And after my skin has been thus destroyed, yet in my flesh I shall see God.

—Job 19:26

What benefits do believers receive from Christ at the resurrection?

At the resurrection, believers are raised up in glory,[1*] openly acknowledged by God, acquitted in the day of judgment,[2] and made perfectly happy in both soul and body[3] in the pleasure of God's company forever.[4]

[1] It is sown in dishonor; it is raised in glory.

—1 Corinthians 15:43

[2] Everyone who acknowledges me before men, I also will acknowledge before my Father who is in heaven.

—Matthew 10:32

[3] When he appears we shall be like him, because we shall see him as he is.

—1 John 3:2

[4] So we will always be with the Lord.

—1 Thessalonians 4:17

[*] *believers are raised up in glory* — that is, raised up in perfection. In heaven, Christians' bodies will be perfect—without defects and deformities. The Lord Jesus Christ "will transform our lowly body to be like his glorious body" (Philippians 3:21).

QUESTION #38

What will happen to the wicked when they die?

When they die, the souls of the wicked will be cast into the torments of hell,[1] and their bodies will remain in their graves until the resurrection and judgment of the great day.[2]

[1] The rich man also died and was buried, and in Hades,* being in torment, he lifted up his eyes and saw Abraham far off and Lazarus at his side. And he called out, "Father Abraham, have mercy on me, and send Lazarus to dip the end of his finger in water and cool my tongue, for I am in anguish in this flame."

—Luke 16:22-24

[2] Like sheep they are appointed for Sheol;** death shall be their shepherd.

—Psalm 49:14

* *Hades* — the place or state of departed souls; a Greek word used for hell in the New Testament.

** *Sheol* — the world of the dead; a Hebrew word used for the grave and hell in the Old Testament.

What will happen to the wicked on the day of judgment?

On the day of judgment, the bodies of the wicked, being raised from their graves, will be sentenced, together with their souls, to inexpressible suffering with the devil and his angels forever.[1]

[1] Many of those who sleep in the dust of the earth shall awake, some to everlasting life, and some to shame and everlasting contempt.

—Daniel 12:2

An hour is coming when all who are in the tombs will hear his voice and come out, those who have done good to the resurrection of life, and those who have done evil to the resurrection of judgment.

—John 5:28-29

They will suffer the punishment of eternal destruction.

—2 Thessalonians 1:9

Depart from me, you cursed, into the eternal fire prepared for the devil and his angels…. These will go away into eternal punishment.

—Matthew 25:41, 46

What did God first give humanity as their rule of law?

The rule of law that God first gave humanity, was the moral law,* which is contained in the Ten Commandments.[1]

[1] He wrote on the tablets, in the same writing as before, the Ten Commandments.

—Deuteronomy 10:4

If you would enter life, keep the commandments.

—Matthew 19:17

* *moral law* — perfect rules for how a person should live.

What is the cornerstone of the Ten Commandments?

The cornerstone* of the Ten Commandments is, to love the Lord our God with all our heart and with all our soul and with all our mind, and our neighbor as ourselves.[1]

[1] And one of them, a lawyer, asked him a question to test him. "Teacher, which is the great commandment in the Law?" And [Jesus] said to him, "You shall love the Lord your God with all your heart and with all your soul and with all your mind. This is the great and first commandment. And a second is like it: You shall love your neighbor as yourself. On these two commandments depend all the Law and the Prophets.

—Matthew 22:35-40

* *cornerstone* — the main stone, especially the one that forms the corner of the foundation of a structure. Jesus answered the lawyer (see proof text above) by giving him the greatest commandments, the most important commandments, of the Law; they are the cornerstone of the Law.

Which is the first commandment?

The first commandment is, "You shall have no other gods before me" (Exodus 20:3).

What is required in the first commandment?

The first commandment requires us to know[1] and acknowledge God as the only true God and our God,[2] and to worship and glorify him appropriately.[3]

[1] And you, Solomon my son, know the God of your father.
—1 Chronicles 28:9

[2] You have declared today that the LORD is your God, and that you will walk in his ways, and keep his statutes and his commandments and his rules, and will obey his voice.
—Deuteronomy 26:17

[3] You shall worship the Lord your God and him only shall you serve.
—Matthew 4:10

Which is the second commandment?

The second commandment is, "You shall not make for yourself a carved image, or any likeness of anything that is in heaven above, or that is in the earth beneath, or that is in the water under the earth. You shall not bow down to them or serve them, for I the LORD your God am a jealous God, visiting the iniquity of the fathers on the children to the third and the fourth generation of those who hate me, but showing steadfast love to thousands of those who love me and keep my commandments" (Exodus 20:4-6).

What is required in the second commandment?

The second commandment requires accepting, observing,[1] and keeping pure, all worship and rules that God has established in his Word.[2]

[1] Take to heart all the words by which I am warning you today, that you may command them to your children, that they may be careful to do all the words of this law.

—Deuteronomy 32:46

Teaching them to observe all that I have commanded you.

—Matthew 28:20

[2] Everything that I command you, you shall be careful to do. You shall not add to it or take from it.

—Deuteronomy 12:32

What is forbidden in the second commandment?

The second commandment forbids worshiping God by means of images,[1] or any other way not established in his Word.[2]

[1] Therefore watch yourselves very carefully. Since you saw no form on the day that the LORD spoke to you at Horeb...lest you act corruptly by making a carved image for yourselves.

—Deuteronomy 4:15-16

[2] Let no one disqualify you, insisting on asceticism and worship of angels, going on in detail about visions, puffed up without reason by his sensuous mind.

—Colossians 2:18

QUESTION #47

Which is the third commandment?

The third commandment is, "You shall not take the name of the LORD your God in vain, for the LORD will not hold him guiltless who takes his name in vain" (Exodus 20:7).

What is required in the third commandment?

The third commandment requires the holy and respectful use of God's names,[1] titles, attributes,[2] ordinances,[3]* Word,[4] and works.[5]

[1] Ascribe to the LORD the glory due his name.

—Psalm 29:2

[2] Great and amazing are your deeds, O Lord God the Almighty! Just and true are your ways, O King of the nations! Who will not fear, O Lord, and glorify your name?

—Revelation 15:3-4

[3] Guard your steps when you go to the house of God. To draw near to listen is better than to offer the sacrifice of fools.

—Ecclesiastes 5:1

[4] I bow down toward your holy temple and give thanks to your name for your steadfast love and your faithfulness, for you have exalted above all things your name and your word.

—Psalm 138:2

[5] Remember to extol his work, of which men have sung.

—Job 36:24

If you are not careful to do all the words of this law that are written in this book, that you may fear this glorious and awesome name, the LORD your God, then the Lord will bring on you and your offspring extraordinary afflictions, afflictions severe and lasting, and sicknesses grievous and lasting.

—Deuteronomy 28:58-59

* *ordinance* — a rule, law, command, ceremony, observance, order, directive, regulation.

Which is the fourth commandment?

The fourth commandment is, "Remember the Sabbath day, to keep it holy. Six days you shall labor, and do all your work, but the seventh day is a Sabbath to the LORD your God. On it you shall not do any work, you, or your son, or your daughter, your male servant, or your female servant, or your livestock, or the sojourner who is within your gates. For in six days the Lord made heaven and earth, the sea, and all that is in them, and rested on the seventh day. Therefore the LORD blessed the Sabbath day and made it holy" (Exodus 20:8-11).

What is required in the fourth commandment?

The fourth commandment requires keeping separated to God such times as he has established in his Word, namely one entire day in seven, to be a holy Sabbath to God.[1]

[1] You shall keep my Sabbaths and reverence my sanctuary: I am the LORD.

—Leviticus 19:30

Observe the Sabbath day, to keep it holy, as the LORD your God commanded you.

—Deuteronomy 5:12

QUESTION #51

How is the Sabbath to be kept separate?

The Sabbath is to be kept separate by making it a day of holy rest, excluding secular employment and recreation that are acceptable on other days,[1] and spending the entire time in public and private worship,[2] except for necessary work and tasks of mercy.[3]

[1] Six days shall work be done, but on the seventh day is a Sabbath of solemn rest, a holy convocation. You shall do no work.

—Leviticus 23:3

[2] A PSALM. A SONG FOR THE SABBATH. It is good to give thanks to the LORD, to sing praises to your name, O Most High; to declare your steadfast love in the morning, and your faithfulness by night.

—Psalm 92:1-2

[3] Which one of you who has a sheep, if it falls into a pit on the Sabbath, will not take hold of it and lift it out? Of how much more value is a man than a sheep! So it is lawful to do good on the Sabbath.

—Matthew 12:11-12

Which is the fifth commandment?

The fifth commandment is, "Honor your father and your mother, that your days may be long in the land that the LORD your God is giving you" (Exodus 20:12).

QUESTION #53

What is required in the fifth commandment?

The fifth commandment requires maintaining honor to everyone, whether higher in position,[1] lower in position,[2] or equal in position,[3] by giving them the proper respect and obedience due them.

[1] Submitting to one another out of reverence for Christ. Wives, submit to your own husbands, as to the Lord.

—Ephesians 5:21-22

Children, obey your parents in the Lord…. Bondservants, obey your earthly masters.

—Ephesians 6:1, 5

Let every person be subject to the governing authorities.

—Romans 13:1

[2] Masters, do the same to them…knowing that he who is both their Master and yours is in heaven.

—Ephesians 6:9

[3] Love one another with brotherly affection. Outdo one another in showing honor.

—Romans 12:10

What reason are we given for obeying the fifth commandment?

The reason given for obeying the fifth commandment is a promise of long life and success—as far as it serves God's glory, and their own good—to all who will keep this commandment.[1]

[1] Honor your father and mother (this is the first commandment with a promise), that it may go well with you and that you may live long in the land.

—Ephesians 6:2-3

Which is the sixth commandment?

The sixth commandment is, "You shall not murder" (Exodus 20:13).

What is forbidden in the sixth commandment?

The sixth commandment forbids, taking our own life,[1] or the life of our neighbor unlawfully,[2] or whatever may contribute to it.[3]

[1] Paul cried with a loud voice, "Do not harm yourself."

—Acts 16.28

[2] Whoever sheds the blood of man, by man shall his blood be shed.

—Genesis 9:6

[3] Rescue those who are being taken away to death; hold back those who are stumbling to the slaughter. If you say, "Behold, we did not know this," does not he who weighs the heart perceive it?

—Proverbs 24:11-12

QUESTION #57

Which is the seventh commandment?

The seventh commandment is, "You shall not commit adultery" (Exodus 20:14).

QUESTION #58

What is forbidden in the seventh commandment?

The seventh commandment forbids engaging in all sexual immorality in thoughts,[1] words,[2] and actions.[3]

[1] Everyone who looks at a woman with lustful intent has already committed adultery with her in his heart.

—Matthew 5:28

[2] Let your speech always be gracious, seasoned with salt, so that you may know how you ought to answer each person.

—Colossians 4:6

Let there be no filthiness nor foolish talk nor crude joking, which are out of place.

—Ephesians 5:4

So flee youthful passions and pursue righteousness, faith, love, and peace, along with those who call on the Lord from a pure heart.

—2 Timothy 2:22

[3] Sexual immorality and all impurity…must not even be named among you.

—Ephesians 5:3

Which is the eighth commandment?

The eighth commandment is, "You shall not steal" (Exodus 20:15).

What is forbidden in the eighth commandment?

The eighth commandment forbids whatever does or may prevent our own,[1] or our neighbor's wealth or success.[2]

[1] If anyone does not provide for his relatives, and especially for members of his household, he has denied the faith and is worse than an unbeliever.

—1 Timothy 5:8

He who follows worthless pursuits will have plenty of poverty.

—Proverbs 28:19

The getting of treasures by a lying tongue is a fleeting vapor and a snare of death.

—Proverbs 21:6

[2] Let the thief no longer steal, but rather let him labor, doing honest work with his own hands, so that he may have something to share with anyone in need.

—Ephesians 4:28

Which is the ninth commandment?

The ninth commandment is, "You shall not bear false witness against your neighbor" (Exodus 20:16).

QUESTION #62

What is required in the ninth commandment?

The ninth commandment requires us to always be truthful,[1] and keep and defend the truth about our own[2] and our neighbor's good name,[3] especially when giving testimony.[4]

[1] Speak the truth to one another.

—Zechariah 8:16

[2] Having a good conscience, so that, when you are slandered, those who revile your good behavior in Christ may be put to shame.

—1 Peter 3:16

But Paul said, "I am standing before Caesar's tribunal…. To the Jews I have done no wrong, as you yourself know very well."

—Acts 25:10

[3] Demetrius has received a good testimony from everyone, and from the truth itself. We also add our testimony, and you know that our testimony is true.

—3 John 12

[4] A faithful witness does not lie…. A truthful witness saves lives.

—Proverbs 14:5, 25

QUESTION #63

Which is the tenth commandment?

The tenth commandment is, "You shall not covet your neighbor's house; you shall not covet your neighbor's wife, or his male servant, or his female servant, or his ox, or his donkey, or anything that is your neighbors" (Exodus 20:17).

QUESTION #64

What is forbidden in the tenth commandment?

The tenth commandment forbids all dissatisfaction with our own situation,[1] envying or being upset over the success of our neighbor,[2] and all excessive thinking about and desiring anything that our neighbor owns.[3]

[1] Nor grumble, as some of them did and were destroyed by the Destroyer.

—1 Corinthians 10:10

[2] Let us not become conceited, provoking one another, envying one another.

—Galatians 5:26

[3] Put to death therefore what is earthly in you: sexual immorality, impurity, passion, evil desire, and covetousness, which is idolatry.

—Colossians 3:5

Is anyone able to keep the commandments of God perfectly?

No mere human, since the fall, is able to keep the commandments of God perfectly in this life,[1] but actually breaks them every day in thought,[2] word,[3] and action.[4]

[1] Surely there is not a righteous man on earth who does good and never sins.

—Ecclesiastes 7:20

[2] The intention of man's heart is evil from his youth.

—Genesis 8:21

[3] No human being can tame the tongue. It is a restless evil, full of deadly poison.

—James 3:8

[4] We all stumble in many ways.

—James 3:2

Is all breaking of the law equally wicked?

Some sins, in their very nature and effect, are worse than others in God's eyes.[1]

[1] Jesus answered him…, "He who delivered me over to you has the greater sin."

—John 19:11

If anyone sees his brother committing a sin not leading to death, he shall ask, and God will give him life—to those who commit sins that do not lead to death. There is sin that leads to death; I do not say that one should pray for that.

—1 John 5:16

What does every sin deserve?

Every sin deserves God's anger, both in this life and the life that is to come.[1]

[1] Let no one deceive you with empty words, for because of these things the wrath of God comes upon the sons of disobedience.

—Ephesians 5:6

Let him rain coals on the wicked; fire and sulfur and a scorching wind shall be the portion of their cup.

—Psalm 11:6

Question #68

How may we escape the anger and curse of God that we deserve due to our sin?

To escape the anger and curse of God that we deserve due to our sin, we must believe in the Lord Jesus Christ,[1] trusting alone to his blood and righteousness. This faith is accompanied by repentance for the past[2] and leads to holiness in the future.

[1] God so loved the world, that he gave his only Son, that whoever believes in him should not perish but have eternal life.

—John 3:16

[2] Testifying both to Jews and to Greeks of repentance toward God and of faith in our Lord Jesus Christ.

—Acts 20:21

What is faith in Jesus Christ?

Faith in Jesus Christ is a saving gift,[1] where we receive,[2] and trust on him alone for salvation,[3] as he is explained in the gospel.[4]

[1] For by grace you have been saved through faith. And this is not your own doing; it is the gift of God.

—Ephesians 2:8

We are not of those who shrink back and are destroyed, but of those who have faith and preserve their souls.

—Hebrews 10:39

[2] To all who did receive him, who believed in his name, he gave the right to become children of God.

—John 1:12

[3] And be found in him, not having a righteousness of my own that comes from the law, but that which comes through faith in Christ, the righteousness from God that depends on faith.

—Philippians 3:9

[4] For the LORD is our judge; the Lord is our lawgiver; the LORD is our king; he will save us.

—Isaiah 33:22

What is repentance that leads to life?

Repentance that leads to life, is a saving gift,[1] by which a sinner, out of a true sense of sin,[2] with hope in the mercy of God through Christ,[3] and with shame and hatred of their sin, turns from their sin to God,[4] with a full determination to strive to obey God.[5]

[1] Then to the Gentiles also God has granted repentance that leads to life.

—Acts 11:18

[2] Now when they heard this they were cut to the heart, and said to Peter and the rest of the apostles, "Brothers, what shall we do?"

—Acts 2:37

[3] Rend your hearts and not your garments. Return to the LORD your God, for he is gracious and merciful, slow to anger, and abounding in steadfast love; and he relents over disaster.

—Joel 2:13

[4] Bring me back that I may be restored, for you are the LORD my God. For after I had turned away, I relented, and after I was instructed, I struck my thigh; I was ashamed, and I was confounded, because I bore the disgrace of my youth.

—Jeremiah 31:18-19

[5] When I think on my ways, I turn my feet to your testimonies.

—Psalm 119:59

QUESTION #71

What are the external and normal ways the Holy Spirit uses to give us the benefits of Christ's redemption?

The external and normal ways the Holy Spirit uses to give us the benefits of redemption, are the Word of God, by which souls are born again to spiritual life, baptism, the Lord's Supper, prayer, and meditation, all of which strengthen believers in their most holy faith.[1]

[1]So those who received his word were baptized.... And they devoted themselves to the apostles' teaching and the fellowship, to the breaking of bread and the prayers.

—Acts 2:41-42

Of his own will he brought us forth by the word of truth.

—James 1:18

QUESTION #72

How is the Word of God used to achieve salvation?

The Spirit of God makes the reading, and especially the preaching of the Word of God, an effective means of convincing and converting sinners,[1] and building them up in holiness and joy,[2] through faith to salvation.[3]

[1] The law of the LORD is perfect, reviving the soul; the testimony of the LORD is sure, making wise the simple.

—Psalm 19:7

[2] You became imitators of us and of the Lord, for you received the word in much affliction, with the joy of the Holy Spirit.

—1 Thessalonians 1:6

[3] I am not ashamed of the gospel, for it is the power of God for salvation to everyone who believes.

—Romans 1:16

QUESTION #73

How is the Word of God to be read and heard to achieve salvation?

For the Word of God to achieve salvation, we must read and listen to it with commitment,[1] preparation,[2] and prayer,[3] receive it with faith[4] and love,[5] store it up in our hearts,[6] and practice it in our lives.[7]

[1] Blessed is the one who listens to me, watching daily at my gates, waiting beside my doors.

—Proverbs 8:34

[2] So put away all malice and all deceit and hypocrisy and envy and all slander. Like newborn infants, long for the pure spiritual milk, that by it you may grow up into salvation.

—1 Peter 2:1-2

[3] Open my eyes, that I may behold wondrous things out of your law.

—Psalm 119:18

[4] For good news came to us just as to them, but the message they heard did not benefit them, because they were not united by faith with those who listened.

—Hebrews 4:2

[5] They refused to love the truth and so be saved.

—2 Thessalonians 2:10

[6] I have stored up your word in my heart, that I might not sin against you.

—Psalm 119:11

[7] But the one who looks into the perfect law, the law of liberty, and perseveres, being no hearer who forgets but a doer who acts, he will be blessed in his doing.

—James 1:25

QUESTION #74

How do baptism and the Lord's Supper become effective instruments of grace?

Baptism and the Lord's Supper become effective instruments of grace, not from any virtue in them, or in the person who administers them,[1] but only by the blessing of Christ,[2] and the working of the Spirit in those who receive them by faith.[3]

[1] So neither he who plants nor he who waters is anything, but only God who gives the growth.

—1 Corinthians 3:7

Baptism, which corresponds to this, now saves you, not as a removal of dirt from the body but as an appeal to God for a good conscience, through the resurrection of Jesus Christ.

—1 Peter 3:21

[2] I planted, Apollos watered, but God gave the growth.

—1 Corinthians 3:6

[3] For in one Spirit we were all baptized into one body—Jews or Greeks, slaves or free—and all were made to drink of one Spirit.

—1 Corinthians 12:13

SPURGEON'S
Catechism

What is baptism?

Baptism is an ordinance* of the New Testament, established by Jesus Christ,[1] as a sign to the person baptized of their relationship to Christ, in his death, burial, and resurrection,[2] of their being grafted** into him,[3] of forgiveness of sins,[4] and of their giving themself to God through Jesus Christ, to live and walk in newness of life.[5]

[1] Go therefore and make disciples of all nations, baptizing them in the name of the Father and of the Son and of the Holy Spirit.
—Matthew 28:19

[2] Do you not know that all of us who have been baptized into Christ Jesus were baptized into his death?
—Romans 6:3

Buried with him in baptism, in which you were also raised with him.
—Colossians 2:12

[3] For as many of you as were baptized into Christ have put on Christ.
—Galatians 3:27

I am the vine; you are the branches. Whoever abides in me and I in him, he it is that bears much fruit, for apart from me you can do nothing.
—John 15:5

[4] John appeared, baptizing in the wilderness and proclaiming a baptism of repentance for the forgiveness of sins.
—Mark 1:4

And now why do you wait? Rise and be baptized and wash away your sins, calling on his name.
—Acts 22:16

[5] We were buried therefore with him by baptism into death, in order that, just as Christ was raised from the dead by the glory of the Father, we too might walk in newness of life. For if we have been united with him in a death like his, we shall certainly be united with him in a resurrection like his.

—Romans 6:4-5

* *ordinance* — a rule, law, command, ceremony, observance, order, directive, regulation.

** *graft* — a shoot or twig inserted into a slit on the trunk or stem of a living plant, from which it receives sap.

Who may be baptized?

Baptism is for all those who actually proclaim repentance* toward God, and faith in our Lord Jesus Christ, and to no one else.[1]

[1] And Peter said to them, "Repent and be baptized every one of you in the name of Jesus Christ for the forgiveness of your sins."

—Acts 2:38

And they were baptized by him in the river Jordan, confessing their sins.

—Matthew 3:6

Whoever believes and is baptized will be saved.

—Mark 16:16

But when they believed Philip as he preached good news about the kingdom of God and the name of Jesus Christ, they were baptized, both men and women.... And as they were going along the road they came to some water, and the eunuch said, "See, here is water! What prevents me from being baptized?" And Philip said, "If you believe with all your heart, you may."

—Acts 8:12, 36-37

"Can anyone withhold water for baptizing these people, who have received the Holy Spirit just as we have?" And he commanded them to be baptized in the name of Jesus Christ.

—Acts 10:47-48

* *repentance* — the pain, regret or sorrow that a person feels because of their past conduct.

Are the infants of parents who claim to be Christians to be baptized?

The infants of parents who claim to be Christians are not to be baptized, because there is not a command nor example in the Holy Scriptures for their baptism.[1]

[1] Pay attention to all that I have said to you.

—Exodus 23:13

Do not add to his words, lest he rebuke you and you be found a liar.

—Proverbs 30:6

How is baptism correctly performed?

Baptism is correctly performed by immersion, or dipping the entire body of the person in water,[1] in the name of the Father, and of the Son, and of the Holy Spirit, according to Christ's example, and the practice of the apostles,[2] and not by the tradition of sprinkling or pouring water, or dipping some part of the body.[3]

[1] And when Jesus was baptized, immediately he went up from the water.

—Matthew 3:16

John also was baptizing at Aenon[*] near Salim,[**] because water was plentiful there, and people were coming and being baptized.

—John 3:23

[2] Go therefore and make disciples of all nations, baptizing them in the name of the Father and of the Son and of the Holy Spirit, teaching them to observe all that I have commanded you. And behold, I am with you always, to the end of the age.

—Matthew 28:19-20

[3] Now when Jesus learned that the Pharisees had heard that Jesus was making and baptizing more disciples than John (although Jesus himself did not baptize, but only his disciples), he left Judea.

—John 4:1-3

And they both went down into the water, Philip and the eunuch, and he baptized him. And when they came up out of the water, the Spirit of the Lord carried Philip away.

—Acts 8:38-39

[*] Aenon — pronounced *ee-non*

[**] Salim — pronounced *sa-leem*

What is the responsibility of those who are baptized according to the will of God?

It is the responsibility of those who are baptized according to the will of God, to join a well-regulated church of Jesus Christ,[1] walk blamelessly before God, and keep all the commandments and ordinances* of the Lord.[2]

[1] The Lord added to their number day by day those who were being saved.

—Acts 2:47

And when he had come to Jerusalem, he attempted to join the disciples.

—Acts 9:26

You yourselves like living stones are being built up as a spiritual house, to be a holy priesthood, to offer spiritual sacrifices acceptable to God through Jesus Christ.

—1 Peter 2:5

[2] And they were both righteous before God, walking blamelessly in all the commandments and statutes of the Lord.

—Luke 1:6

* *ordinance* — a rule, law, command, ceremony, observance, order, directive, regulation.

Question #80

What is the Lord's Supper?

The Lord's Supper is an ordinance of the New Testament, established by Jesus Christ; in which, by giving and receiving bread and wine, according to his instruction, his death is portrayed,[1] and those, who are deserving by faith, share in the benefits of his body and blood, through personal spiritual nourishment, and growth in grace.[2]

[1] For I received from the Lord what I also delivered to you, that the Lord Jesus on the night when he was betrayed took bread, and when he had given thanks, he broke it, and said, "This is my body, which is for you. Do this in remembrance of me." In the same way also he took the cup, after supper, saying, "This cup is the new covenant in my blood. Do this, as often as you drink it, in remembrance of me." For as often as you eat this bread and drink the cup, you proclaim the Lord's death until he comes.

—1 Corinthians 11:23-26

[2] The cup of blessing that we bless, is it not a participation in the blood of Christ? The bread that we break, is it not a participation in the body of Christ?

—1 Corinthians 10:16

QUESTION #81

What is required to participate in the Lord's Supper?

It is required of those who would properly receive the Lord's Supper, that they understand the meaning of the Lord's body,[1] know they are in the faith,[2] are repentant of their sins,[3] love the household of faith,[4] and receive the Supper with a clear conscience before God,[5] to avoid the risk of bringing judgment on themselves.[6]

[1] Let a person examine himself, then, and so eat of the bread and drink of the cup. For anyone who eats and drinks without discerning the body eats and drinks judgment on himself.
—1 Corinthians 11:28-29

[2] Examine yourselves, to see whether you are in the faith.
—2 Corinthians 13:5

[3] If we judged ourselves truly, we would not be judged.
—1 Corinthians 11:31

[4] When you come together as a church, I hear that there are divisions among you…. When you come together, it is not the Lord's supper that you eat.
—1 Corinthians 11: 18, 20

[5] Let us therefore celebrate the festival, not with the old leaven, the leaven of malice and evil, but with the unleavened bread of sincerity and truth.
—1 Corinthians 5:8

[6] Whoever, therefore, eats the bread or drinks the cup of the Lord in an unworthy manner will be guilty concerning the body and blood of the Lord…. Anyone who eats and drinks without discerning the body eats and drinks judgment on himself.
—1 Corinthians 11:27, 29

What is meant by the words, "until he comes,"* that are used by the apostle Paul regarding the Lord's Supper?

They clearly teach us that our Lord Jesus Christ will come a second time. This is the joy and hope of all believers.[1]

[1] This Jesus, who was taken up from you into heaven, will come in the same way as you saw him go into heaven.

—Acts 1:11

For the Lord himself will descend from heaven with a cry of command, with the voice of an archangel, and with the sound of the trumpet of God. And the dead in Christ will rise first.

—1 Thessalonians 4:16

* For as often as you eat this bread and drink the cup, you proclaim the Lord's death <u>until he comes</u>. —1 Corinthians 11:26

A Letter to the Reader

[Adapted from Mr. Spurgeon's book *All of Grace*.]

I hope working through this catechism and reading this letter will help you to find peace with God. My goal is that you will find Christ and heaven. God has seen to it that you have this catechism. Have you given your attention to these questions and answers? Will you give your attention to this letter written to you? Who knows, perhaps they will be a blessing for you.

I heard a story. A pastor called on a poor woman, intending to give her help, because he knew she was very poor. He knocked at the door, with his money in hand, but she did not answer. He assumed she was not at home and went his way. Later, he met her at the church and told her that he had remembered her need. "I called at your house, and knocked several times, and I assumed you were not at home, because there was no answer." "What time did you call, pastor?" "It was about noon." "Oh, dear," she said, "I heard you, pastor. I am so sorry I did not answer, but I thought it was the landlord calling for the rent."

I hope you will not be like that woman. I am not seeking anything for myself by writing this to you. I only want to help you. I want you to know that salvation is all by grace. That means it is free, without charge, for nothing! I am not going to tell you that God demands that you keep his rules. Like the woman in that story who could not pay her landlord and pretended that she was not home, you know you should obey God's laws, but that you can't. No, I am not coming to make demands on you, but to bring you something. We are not going to talk about law, and duty, and punishment, but about love, goodness, forgiveness, mercy, and eternal life.

Do not act like you are not at home. Do not pretend you can't hear me, do not have a careless heart. I am not asking anything from you in the name of God or anyone else. It is not my intention to require anything from you. I come in God's name to bring you a free gift. A gift that will bring you joy now and for eternity.

Open the door and let my words come in. The Lord himself invites you to a meeting about your immediate and endless happiness. He says, "Come now, let us reason together." He would not have said this if he did not have your best interests at heart. Do not refuse the Lord Jesus who knocks at your door. He knocks with a hand that was nailed to the cross for people like you. His only purpose is for your good, so listen to him and come to him.

Listen carefully and let the good word of God sink into your soul. Perhaps this is the hour that you will enter into that new life that is the beginning of heaven. Faith comes by hearing and reading is a sort of hearing. Faith may come to you while you are reading this letter. Why not! Oh blessed Spirit of all grace, make it happen!

God is Speaking to You

Here is a message from God to you: "To the one who does not work but trusts him who justifies the ungodly, his faith is counted as righteousness." That means that God is like a judge who says to a defendant, "Not guilty." Are you surprised the Bible has an expression like that? God "justifies the ungodly." He makes those who are guilty innocent. He forgives those who deserve to be punished. He favors those who deserve no favor. You thought, didn't you, that salvation was for good people?

Did you think that God's grace was for the pure and holy, for those who are free from sin? Have you thought that if you were excellent, then God would reward you? Do you think that because you are not worthy, that there is no way you could enjoy God's favor? You must be somewhat surprised to read a passage like this: "Him who justifies the ungodly." I am not surprised that you are surprised, because, as familiar as I am with the great grace of God, I never cease to be amazed by it.

It does sound surprising, doesn't it, that it is possible for a holy God to justify an unholy person? Our hearts naturally tend to think we must do what God tells us and not do what he forbids before we can please him. We are always talking about our own goodness and our own worthiness, and stubbornly believe that we must somehow measure up if we expect to win God's notice. But we are only fooling ourselves. God knows that there is no goodness whatever in any of us. He says, "None is righteous, no, not one." He knows that "all our righteous deeds are like a polluted garment." The Lord Jesus did not come into the world to find goodness and righteousness. He came to give them to people who have none. He does not come because we are innocent, but to make us innocent. He justifies the ungodly.

When an attorney comes into court, if they are an honest person, they want to plead the case of an innocent person and justify them before the court. They want to prove that the charges against their client are false. The lawyer's goal should be to justify the innocent person and they should not attempt to protect those who are guilty. No human being has the right, and they should not have the power, to justify the guilty. This is a miracle that is reserved for the Lord alone.

God knows that there is not a righteous person on the earth that does good and does not sin. Therefore, in his inexpressible love, he takes on the job of justifying the ungodly. God has come up with the ways and means of making the ungodly person able to stand before him as an innocent person. He has worked out a system, with perfect justice. He can treat the guilty as if they had been completely free of sin their entire life. He justifies the ungodly.

Jesus Christ came into the world to save *sinners*. That is a very surprising thing. And the people who are most amazed by it are those who actually have and enjoy his salvation. I know that to me, even after all these years, this is the greatest wonder I have ever heard—that God would ever justify *me*. I feel like I am a lump of unworthiness and a heap of sin, without his almighty love. God has assured me that I am justified by faith in Christ Jesus and treats me as if I have always been perfect and righteous. He has made me a child of God, and yet I know that without God's grace I must be included among the most sinful. I am completely undeserving, and yet he treats me as if I had been deserving. I am loved with as much love as if I had always been a godly person, when the truth is, I was ungodly. Who can help being amazed at this?

This is very surprising, but I want you to notice how available it makes the gospel to you and me. If God justifies the *ungodly*, then, dear friend, he can justify *you*. Are you ungodly? Are you unconverted right now? Then you really are ungodly—even if you are better than some other people. You have lived without God. You have been the opposite of godly. In one word, you have been and are *ungodly*.

Perhaps you have not gone to church on Sundays or read the Bible. That would make you ungodly. But perhaps you have, but your heart is not in it. That would also make you ungodly. You have never met God personally. You do not love God in your heart and you have not obeyed his commands.

Well, if this is the case, then you are just the kind of person to whom this gospel is sent. God says that he justifies *the ungodly*. It is a wonderful gospel, and, happily, it is available for you. It just suits you, doesn't it? How I wish that you would accept it!

Real Sinners Can Be Saved

If you realize that you are a sinner and are willing to admit it, that is the very reason why you can be saved. You are a sinner, and if you do not trust in the Lord Jesus Christ, then you are lost forever. But Jesus "came to seek and to save the lost." He died and paid the price for sin for real sinners. If you acknowledge that you are a sinner, God's grace is available to you.

The person who understands they are a filthy sinner is the very type of person Jesus Christ came to make clean. His salvation is for sinners, for those who are lost and guilty. Do not be afraid because you think you must be good enough before God will accept you. He will cheerfully forgive you, not because you are good, but because *he is* good. Jesus Christ came into the world to save sinners. Forgiveness is for the guilty.

Do not attempt to touch yourself up and make yourself something that you are really not. Come to the God who justifies the ungodly just as they are. A great artist was commissioned to paint the people who made the city work. For historic reasons, he wanted to include certain well-known people of the town in his picture. One person to be included was a handyman who was known to everyone in the town. He was always seen around the city wearing his filthy, untidy, worn-out clothes, begging for odd jobs, but the artist felt he must be included. He said to this ragged and rugged individual, "I will pay you well if you will come down to my studio and let me paint your likeness."

He came around in the morning, but he was soon sent out the door, because he had washed his face, combed his hair, and was wearing a respectable suit of clothes. He was needed as a beggar and was not invited in any other position. In the same way, Jesus will receive you into his house if you come as a sinner and no other way. Do not wait until you have changed your ways. Come now and come as you are for salvation. God justifies *the ungodly*. God takes you where you are right now, in your worst condition.

Come in your filthy worn-out clothes. I mean, come to your heavenly Father in all your sin and sinfulness. Come to Jesus just as you are, even if you think you are not fit to live. Come, even though you hardly dare to hope for anything except God's judgment. Come and ask the Lord to justify another ungodly person. Why should he not justify you? Come, because this great mercy of God is meant for people like you.

Do not put off thinking about this very seriously.

God Justifies Ungodly People

Only God can justify the ungodly, and he can do it perfectly. He throws our sins behind his back. He blots them out. He says that even if they are searched for, they will not be found. Why? There is no other reason for it except his own wonderful goodness. We are not talking about God dealing with people according to what they deserve. Our great God is able to treat guilty people with great mercy. He is able to treat ungodly people as if they had always been godly.

The greatest fact under heaven is this: Christ, by his precious blood actually puts sin away. And God, for Christ's sake, deals with people with divine mercy, forgives the guilty and justifies them—not according to anything good he sees in them, or sees will be in them in the future, but according to the riches of his mercy that come from his own heart.

Friend, *the Lord can blot out all your sins.* I am not just guessing when I say, "Every sin and blasphemy will be forgiven people" (Matthew 12:31). If you are up to your neck in crime, he can remove the contamination by saying, "I will you to be clean." The Lord is a great forgiver.

"Well," you say, "it would be a great miracle if the Lord pardoned me." Yes, it would be! It would be a marvelous miracle and therefore he is likely to do it. He "does great things and unsearchable, marvelous things without number" (Job 5:9).

I was once afflicted with a horrible sense of guilt. My life was miserable; but then I heard the command, "Turn to me and be saved, all the ends of the earth! For I am God, and there is no other" (Isaiah 45:22). I turned, and in a moment the Lord justified me. I saw Jesus Christ, made sin for me, and that sight gave me peace.

The Holy Spirit gave me the will to believe and gave me peace through believing. I felt just as sure that I was forgiven as I had previously felt that I was condemned. The Bible told me that I was condemned, and so did my conscience. But the Bible says,

"Whoever believes in him is not condemned" (John 3:18), and my conscience believed that God could pardon me.

Oh, how I wish that you would accept God's word about this. If you would, then your own conscience would soon be at peace.

What Is Believing In Jesus?

What does it mean to believe in Jesus? It is not merely to say, "He is God and the Savior." It is to trust him completely and absolutely, to take him as the payment for your salvation from this time on and forever, and take him as your Lord, your Master, your everything.

If you will have Jesus, he has you already. If you believe in him, I tell you, you cannot go to hell. That would make Christ's sacrifice meaningless.

Every believer can claim that Christ's sacrifice was actually made for them. By faith, the believer in Christ has taken the Lamb of God and made him their own. Therefore they can never perish. The Lord cannot read our pardon written in the blood of his own Son and then punish us. That is impossible. Oh that you may have the grace given you to look right now to Jesus.

Your life is like a sinking ship and Jesus is the lifeboat where you can be safe. People do not bring things with them when their ship is sinking. They leap from the ship and swim to the lifeboat just as they are and as fast as they can. Will you come into this lifeboat, just as you are?

I will tell you this thing about myself to encourage you. My only hope for heaven lies in the full atonement made on Calvary's cross for the ungodly. I rely on that firmly. I do not have the shadow of a hope anywhere else. You are in the same condition as me. Neither of us have anything of our own worth trusting in. Let us join hands and stand together at the foot of the cross and trust our souls once and for all to him who shed his blood for the guilty. We will be saved by the same Savior. If you perish trusting him, I must perish also. What more can I do to prove my own confidence in the gospel I am telling you about?

We Are Saved by Grace

The Bible says, "By grace you have been saved through faith" (Ephesians 2:8). Salvation is by the grace of God. We are not saved because of anything we do or can do. We are not saved because of anything in us, or that ever can be in us. It is because of the limitless love, goodness, pity, compassion, mercy and grace of God.

God's grace is immense. Who can measure its width? Who can find its bottom? Like everything else about God, his grace is infinite. God is full of love, because "God is love." God is full of goodness— "God" is short for "good." Unlimited goodness and love are part of the very essence of God. It is because "his steadfast love endures forever" that people are not destroyed. It is because "his mercies never come to an end" that sinners are brought to him and forgiven.

Do not become focused on faith. As essential as faith is, it is only an important part of the machinery that grace uses. We are saved "through faith," but salvation is "by grace." "By grace you have been saved." You see, a weak faith will not destroy you. What glad news for we who do not deserve God's love! Look only to Jesus.

What Is Faith?

What is faith? It is made up of three things—knowledge, belief, and trust. Knowledge comes first. I need to be informed about something before I can possibly believe it. "Faith comes from hearing." We must hear first, so that we may know what we are to believe. Knowledge is important, because a certain amount of knowledge is essential to faith. "Incline your ear, and come to me; hear, that your soul may live." These are the words of the ancient prophet Isaiah and they are still true today.

After knowledge, the mind goes on to *believe* that these things are true. The soul believes that God is real and that he hears the cries of sincere hearts. It believes that the gospel is from God and that justification by faith is the great truth that God has revealed by his Spirit. Then the heart truly believes that Jesus is our God and Savior; that he is the Redeemer of people—the Prophet, Priest, and King of his people. All of this must be accepted as real truth, it must not be called into question. I pray that you may come to this conclusion right now. Believe "the blood of Jesus his Son cleanses us from all sin." Get to the place where you believe it strongly. Believe that his sacrifice is complete and fully accepted by God for you. Believe that anyone who believes in Jesus is not condemned. Believe these truths like you believe any other facts. Believe what God says just like you would believe your own parent or friend.

So far you have been approaching faith. Only one more ingredient is needed to complete it. That is *trust*. Commit yourself to the merciful God. Place all your hope on his gracious gospel. Trust your soul to the dying and living Savior. Wash away your sins in the atoning blood. Accept Christ's perfect righteousness and everything will be okay. Trust is the essential part of faith. There is no saving faith without it. Lean on Christ. Commit yourself to him. That is what faith means. Faith is not something that is blind, because faith begins with knowledge. Faith does not accept unproven theories, because faith believes in facts of which it is certain. Faith is not an impractical thing of dreams, because faith risks everything on the truth of the Bible. That is one way of describing what faith is.

Let me try again. Faith is believing that Christ is what he says he is, that he will do what he has promised to do, and then to expect him to do it. The Bible says that Jesus Christ is God, God in human flesh; it says that his character was perfect, that he became a sin offering for us, and that he bore our sins in his body on the cross. The Bible goes on to say he "died for our sins," "was raised on the third day," that he "always lives to make intercession for" us, and that he has gone up to heaven. We need to believe these things, because this is what God the Father meant when he said, "This is my beloved Son, listen to him."

Faith also believes that Christ will do what he has promised. Faith believes Jesus when he promised, "Whoever comes to me I will never cast out." Whatever Christ has promised to do he will do. We must believe this and look to him for pardon, justification, safekeeping, and eternal glory, because of the promises he has made to those who believe in him.

Then comes the next necessary step. Faith believes that Jesus is what the Bible says he is and that Jesus will do what he says he will do. Each person must trust Jesus to be what he says he is and believe he will do what he has promised to do for everyone who believes in him. Faith is placing yourself in the hands of Jesus, believing that he can save those who believe in him. Faith believes his promise that he will do just what he says he will. This is saving faith and the person who has it has everlasting life. Whatever dangers and difficulties you face, whatever darkness and depression you may experience, whatever your weaknesses and sins, if you believe in Christ Jesus in this way, then you are not condemned, and you will never be sent to hell.

I trust this explanation has helped and that the Spirit of God will use it to bring you immediate peace. "Do not fear, only believe." Trust, and be at peace.

Do not be satisfied with understanding what needs to be done and yet never do it. The poorest real faith in the heart is better than having the best understanding but not doing anything.

Oh dear reader, receive the Lord Jesus into your soul and you will live forever! "WHOEVER BELIEVES IN THE SON HAS ETERNAL LIFE."

How Can We Illustrate Faith?
I will give you a few illustrations to explain more clearly what faith is. Only the Holy Spirit can make you understand, but it is

my job and my joy to provide all the help I can, and to ask the Lord to open your eyes.

The ways people make their living illustrates faith in many ways. The farmer buries good seed in the earth and expects it to not only grow but also to increase. They have faith that a harvest is coming and they are rewarded for their faith.

The retailer deposits their money in the bank and trusts that it will be there when they need it.

Swimmers have faith that the water will keep them buoyant and that they will not sink. They could not swim if they did not have faith to completely plunge into the water.

Goldsmiths put precious metal into the furnace that seems eager to consume it, but they receive it back again from the furnace purified by the heat.

You cannot turn anywhere in life without seeing faith in action. Now, just as we trust in our daily lives, we are to trust in Christ Jesus.

Every child who goes to school has to exercise faith while learning. Their teacher instructs them in geography, and teaches them about the earth, and the existence of certain great cities and empires. The student does not personally know these things are true, but they believe their teacher and the textbooks. That is what you will have to do with Christ if you are to be saved. You must simply know because he tells you, believe because he assures you it is true, and trust yourself with him because he promises you that salvation will be the result.

Almost everything that you and I know has come to us by faith. A scientific discovery has been made and we are sure of it. Why? On the authority of certain well-known scientists whose reputations are respected. We have never made or seen their experiments, but we believe what they tell us. You must do the same regarding Jesus. You are to trust yourself with him. He is worthy to be your Master and Lord. If you will receive him and his words you will be saved.

Why do children trust their father? The reason why a child trusts their father is because they love him. If you love Jesus, you will trust him.

Faith obeys. When a traveler trusts a guide to take them over a difficult pass, they follow the path that their guide points out. When a patient believes in a doctor, they carefully follow their prescriptions and directions. Faith that refuses to obey the commands of the Savior is false faith. It will never save the soul. We trust Jesus to save us; he gives us directions how to be saved; we follow those directions and are saved. Dear reader, do not forget this. Trust Jesus and prove your trust by doing whatever he instructs you.

Will my reader put their trust in God, in Christ Jesus? Believe our heavenly Father and our Savior. Believe in Jesus now.

CATECHISM GLOSSARY

cornerstone — the main stone, especially the one that forms the corner of the foundation of a structure.

covenant — a formal agreement between two or more parties, a contract, a promise.

decree — an official order issued by a legal authority, the legal ruling of a judge. "In those days a *decree* went out from Caesar Augustus that all the world should be registered" (Luke 2:1). God has predetermined, for his own glory, everything that will happen.

foreordain — to ordain, appoint, or decree beforehand; to predestinate; to predetermine.

glorify — to praise, honor in worship, honor in thoughts or words, adore, give thanks to.

graft — a shoot or twig inserted into a slit on the trunk or stem of a living plant, from which it receives sap.

Hades — the place or state of departed souls; a Greek word used for hell in the New Testament.

intercession — prayer to God for, or on behalf of, someone else.

moral law — perfect rules for how a person should live.

neutral soul — a soul like Adam's before the fall.

ordinance — a rule, law, command, ceremony, observance, order, directive, regulation.

propitiation — The act of satisfying someone's demands and changing that someone from an enemy into a friend. When Jesus Christ died on the cross he satisfied the demand of God the Father that a sacrifice for sin must be made to him. The wrath or anger of God was used up on Christ so that God's justice was satisfied and we who were once the enemies of God became his friends.

providence — refers to God's will, his divine intervention, and his predetermination (predestination).

repentance — the pain, regret or sorrow that a person feels because of their past conduct.

Sheol — the world of the dead; a Hebrew word used for the grave and hell in the Old Testament.

state — the particular condition that someone or something is in at a specific time. Condition, situation, position.

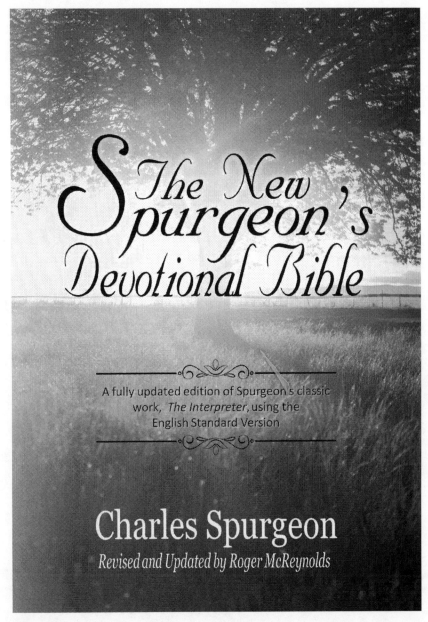

The New Spurgeon's Devotional Bible

A fully updated edition of Spurgeon's classic work, *The Interpreter*, using the English Standard Version

Charles Spurgeon

Revised and Updated by Roger McReynolds

The New Spurgeon's Devotional Bible is a 600,000-word, two year, daily devotional for use in family worship time. This unabridged edition has been fully Updated for Today's Readers; Scripture is in the English Standard Version.

Available in paperback and eBook editions at Amazon.com.

Made in United States
Orlando, FL
07 October 2024

52450565R00071